SRA

Reading Mastery®

Transformations

Reading
Textbook B

Siegfried Engelmann

Owen Engelmann

Karen Davis

McGraw
Hill

Acknowledgments

The authors are grateful to the following people for their assistance in the preparations of Reading Mastery Transformations Grade K Reading.

Joanna Jachowicz
Blake Engelmann
Charlene Tolles-Engelmann
Cally Dwyer
Melissa Morrow
Toni Reeves

Emily Jachowicz for her valuable student input.

We'd also like to acknowledge, from McGraw Hill, the valuable contributions by:

Mary Eisele
Nancy Stigers
Jason Yanok

mheducation.com/prek-12

Send all inquiries to:
McGraw-Hill Education
8787 Orion Place
Columbus, OH 43240

ISBN: 978-0-07-905401-2
MHID: 0-07-905401-3

Printed in the United States of America.

2 3 4 5 6 7 8 9 10 LWI 26 25 24 23 22 21

ai t d y p p th oa

1. <u>th</u>at
2. <u>th</u>e
3. ma<u>th</u>

1. p<u>ai</u>l
2. pal
3. pal mole
4. late

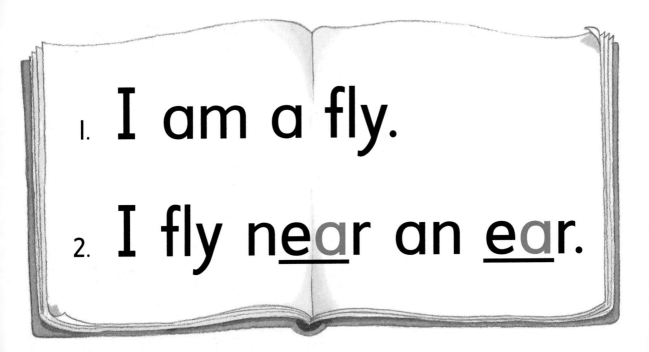

1. I am a fly.

2. I fly n<u>ea</u>r an <u>ea</u>r.

① I am a fly.

near
ear
am
fly

3

ea

oa

ai   th

1. mile

2. time

1. <u>th</u>e

2. <u>th</u>at   3. rop<u>e</u>   4. m<u>e</u>a<u>l</u>

4

1. I rope a ram.
2. See my pal fly.

I rope a ram.

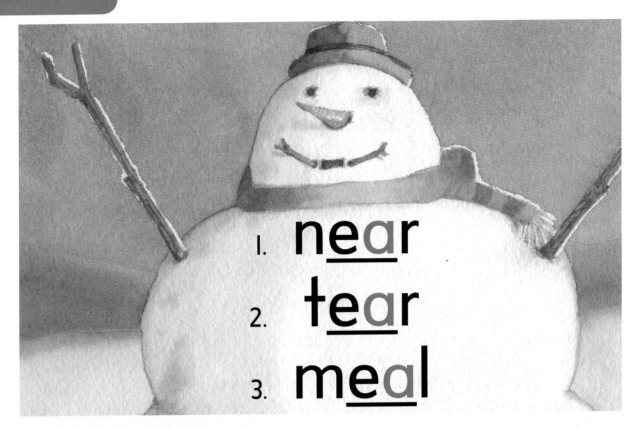

1. n**ea**r
2. t**ea**r
3. m**ea**l

1. an
2. man
3. **th**at

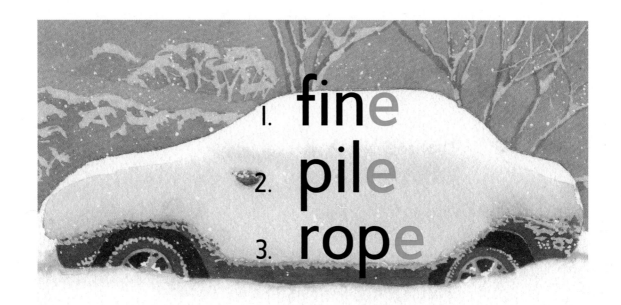

1. fine
2. pile
3. rope

1. I see <u>the</u> man fly.

2. I <u>ea</u>t a m<u>ea</u>l.

1

I see <u>the</u> man fly.

2

I <u>ea</u>t a m<u>ea</u>l.

8

t
p
d
n
th
y

i a

1. time
2. mile

1. <u>th</u>at
2. pa<u>th</u>

1. r<u>ea</u>d
2. dad

1. nam<u>e</u>   2. map

<u>Th</u>e ram ran at <u>th</u>e man. So <u>th</u>at man ran for a mil<u>e</u>.

<u>Th</u>e ram ran at <u>th</u>e man.

So <u>th</u>at man ran
for a mile.

a i t p d y r

1. pile   2. time

1. dad
2. r<u>oa</u>d
3. made

1. saf<u>e</u>
2. rat
3. pa<u>th</u>
4. nam<u>e</u>

A rat ran at a mol<u>e</u>. So <u>th</u>at mole ran n<u>ea</u>r a pil<u>e</u>.

A rat ran at a mole.

So <u>th</u>at mole ran
n<u>ea</u>r a pile.

a i

1. in
2. sit
3. did

1. ma<u>th</u>
2. <u>th</u>at

1. made
2. and
3. t<u>a</u>il

I sat n<u>ea</u>r a
t<u>a</u>il. I made
a rope.

1. **as**
2. **<u>th</u>ose**

i
a

1. **fin**
2. **did**

1. **f<u>oa</u>m**   2. **s<u>oa</u>p**

1. made
2. and

I see f<u>oa</u>m and
a t<u>ai</u>l. I see no
s<u>oa</u>p n<u>ea</u>r me.

1. it
2. pile
3. pill
4. <u>th</u>is
5. time

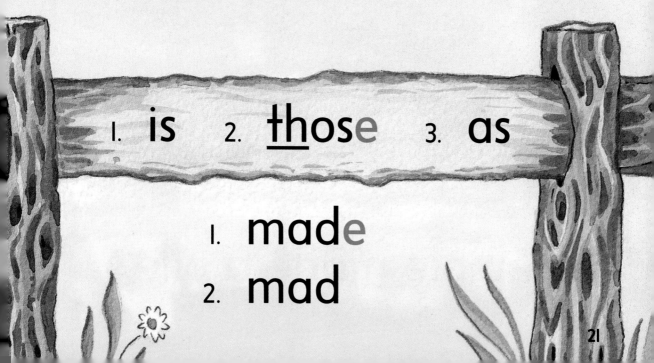

1. is   2. <u>th</u>ose   3. as

1. made
2. mad

A mole made a pile.
<u>Th</u>at pile made <u>the</u>
ram mad.

A mole made a pile.

<u>Th</u>at pile made <u>the</u> ram mad.

1. is
2. as
3. <u>th</u>ese

1. try
2. fly
3. dry

1. time
2. <u>th</u>is
3. did

I see rain. So it is time for math.

d t v k

1. and
2. **th**ose
3. **th**ese
4. **th**at

1. s**ay**
2. d**ay**
3. m**ay**

1. sit
2. sat
3. fine
4. same
5. dad
6. did

1. safe
2. pal
3. my

I sit n<u>ea</u>r my pal. <u>Th</u>at pal is my dad.

v   d

k   j

1. tape
2. tap
3. pin
4. pine

1. try
2. l<u>ay</u>
3. pl<u>ay</u>

a
i

1. in
2. an
3. did

1. time
2. sit
3. m<u>ai</u>l
4. <u>th</u>at

It is time for t<u>he</u> m<u>ai</u>l. <u>Th</u>at m<u>ai</u>l is for me. My s<u>oa</u>p is in <u>th</u>at m<u>ai</u>l.

1. made
2. time
3. r<u>ai</u>n
4. pile

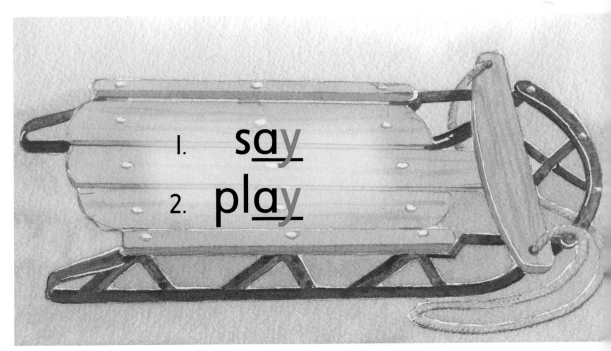

1. s<u>ay</u>
2. pl<u>ay</u>

1. in
2. ant
3. sit
4. <u>th</u>at

<u>Th</u>e r<u>ai</u>n made a ram sit. So <u>th</u>at ram is mad.

34

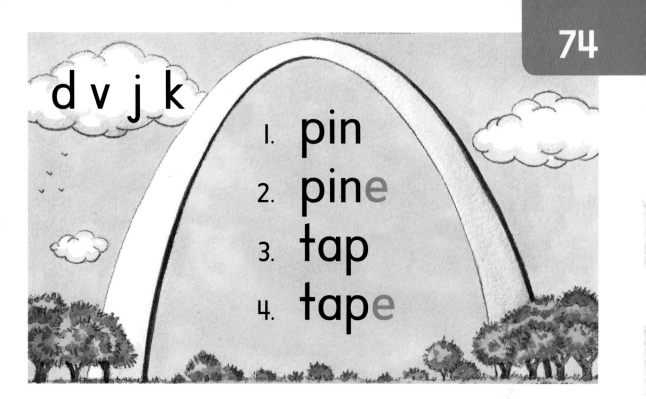

d v j k

1. pin
2. pine
3. tap
4. tape

1. my
2. m<u>ay</u>
3. pl<u>ay</u>

1. an
2. and
3. sat
4. sit

My s_o_ap is in t_he_
m_ai_l. R_ai_n mad_e_ t_ha_t
s_o_ap f_oa_m. An ant is
in t_he_ f_oa_m.

My s_o_ap is
in t_he_ m_ai_l.

Rain made that soap foam.

An ant is in the foam.

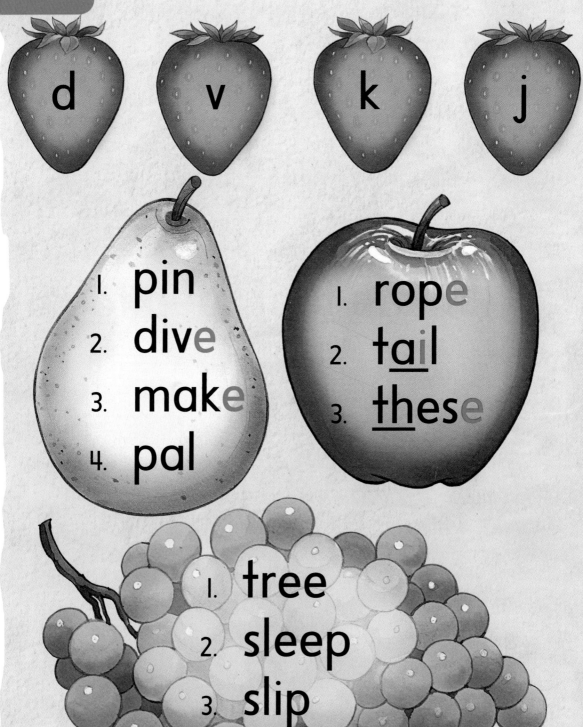

d　　v　　k　　j

1. pin
2. dive
3. make
4. pal

1. rope
2. t<u>ai</u>l
3. <u>th</u>ese

1. tree
2. sleep
3. slip

Sam may eat a rope. That rope is no rope. It is a tail.

I may eat that rope.

k v **ck** j c

1. **th**an
2. and
3. ant

1. mak**e**
2. sav**e**
3. lik**e**
4. j**ai**l
5. van

1. tree
2. trip
3. sleep

A s**ea**l and a ram m**ay** pl**ay**. Or **the** s**ea**l m**ay** sleep. And **the** ram m**ay** **e**at a s**ai**l.

A seal may sleep.

A ram may eat a sail.

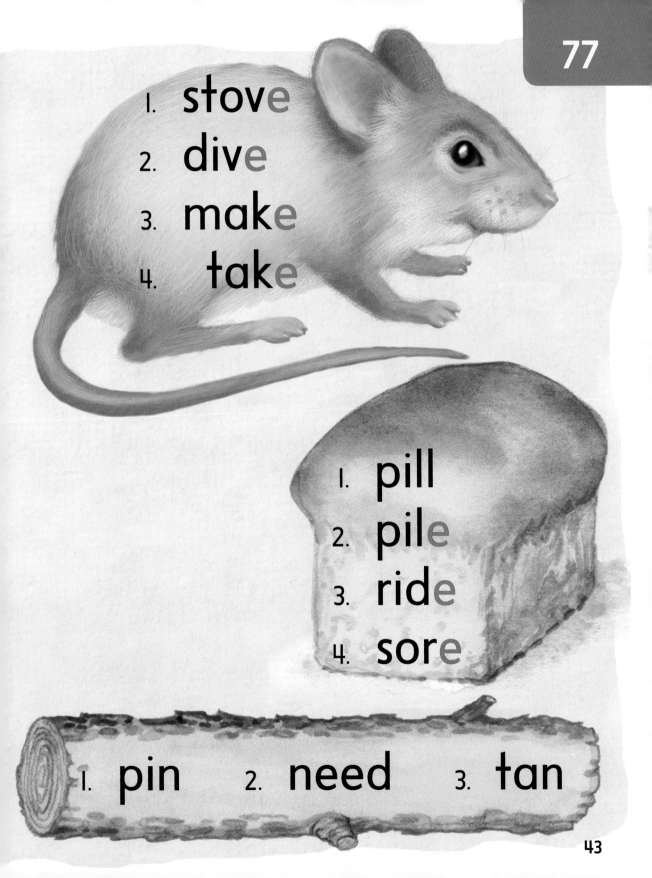

1. stove
2. dive
3. make
4. take

1. pill
2. pile
3. ride
4. sore

1. pin   2. need   3. tan

I see r<u>ai</u>n. My pal m<u>ay</u> pl<u>ay</u> in <u>the</u> r<u>ai</u>n. Or my pal m<u>ay</u> <u>ea</u>t.

I see r<u>ai</u>n.

My pal m<u>ay</u> pl<u>ay</u> in
<u>the</u> r<u>ai</u>n.

Or my pal m<u>ay</u> <u>ea</u>t.

1. j<u>ai</u>l
2. stove
3. like
4. take

1. fine
2. fin
3. sore
4. ride

1. seed
2. need
3. tan

I like my pal. My pal may take me for a ride. That may make me sore.

I like my pal.

My pal m<u>ay</u> take me
for a ride.

<u>Th</u>at m<u>ay</u> make me sore.

c
v
k
j
ck
p

1. take
2. lake
3. joke
4. stove

1. old
2. drive
3. trip

1. pine
2. sleep
3. pa<u>th</u>

An ant is in a pine tree. Is <u>th</u>at ant safe? No.

An ant is in a pine tree.

Is <u>th</u>at ant safe?

th
ck
ay

c   j   k

i   a

1. pins
2. jokes
3. vans

1. cat
2. si<u>ck</u>
3. rake
4. cold

1. old
2. sold
3. store
4. drive

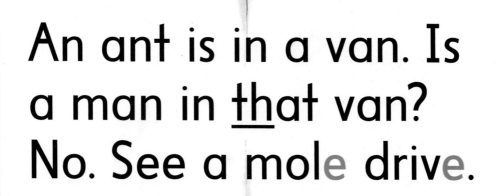

An ant is in a van. Is a man in <u>th</u>at van? No. See a mole drive.

An ant is in a van.

Is a man in <u>th</u>e van?
No. See a mole drive.

ck ay c j v

1. lakes
2. stores
3. trees

1. can
2. day
3. stay

1. lip
2. slip

1. low   2. slow   3. you

Is a rat near the lake?
No. Is the rat in this
tree? No. Is that rat
in a store?

Is a rat near the lake?

Is <u>the</u> rat in <u>th</u>is tree?

<u>Th</u>at rat is in a store.

j   ay   ck   v

1. lakes
2. rakes
3. j<u>ai</u>ls
4. <u>t</u><u>ai</u>ls

1. p<u>ay</u>
2. st<u>ay</u>
3. cat
4. nap

1. old
2. told
3. cold

1. low
2. flow
3. you

Did <u>th</u>e tan ram sleep?
No. Did <u>th</u>at ram dive
in a lake? No. Did <u>th</u>at
ram sit in <u>th</u>e pa<u>th</u>? No.

Did <u>th</u>e tan ram sleep?

Did <u>th</u>at ram dive in a lake?

60

Did <u>th</u>e tan ram sit in
<u>th</u>e pa<u>th</u>?

84

1. cats
2. rakes
3. pals
4. naps

1. know
2. no
3. slow
4. those

1. dime 2. kite 3. lid

A s<u>ea</u>l and 3 pals sat n<u>ea</u>r a lake. <u>Th</u>ose pals m<u>ay</u> pl<u>ay</u> in <u>the</u> lake. Or <u>th</u>ose pals m<u>ay</u> take a nap.

A s<u>ea</u>l and 3 pals sat n<u>ea</u>r a lake.

<u>Th</u>ose pals m<u>ay</u> pl<u>ay</u>
in <u>the</u> lake.

Or <u>th</u>ose pals m<u>ay</u>
take a nap.

85

1. will
2. wi<u>th</u>
3. wide
4. we

i   a

1. ki<u>ck</u>s
2. kites
3. cats
4. c<u>oa</u>ts

1. <u>th</u>ese
2. <u>th</u>ose
3. pa<u>th</u>
4. trip

A rake is in a path.
Cats play in that path.
Did the rake trip those
cats? No. These cats
can eat rakes.

A rake is in a path.

Cats pl<u>ay</u> in <u>th</u>at pa<u>th</u>.

Did <u>the</u> rake trip <u>tho</u>se cats? No. <u>Th</u>ese cats can <u>ea</u>t rakes.

1. you
2. if
3. cats
4. store
5. tr<u>a</u>in

1. sad
2. mad
3. made
4. make

1. win
2. will
3. wide

this

with

A man is near a lake.
A cat will trip that man.
Will that make the man
mad? You will see.

A man is near a lake.

A cat will trip that man.

That made the man mad.

1. deep
2. keep
3. you
4. know

1. made
2. make
3. five
4. snow

1. said
2. trip
3. will

1. those
2. that

Cats ran in a store. A man made those cats sit. Did that make the cats mad? You will see.

Cats ran in a store.

A man made those cats sit. Did that make the cats mad?

g
c
w

1. said
2. over
3. snow
4. deep
5. we

1. needs
2. seeds
3. rakes
4. makes

1. seals
2. cold
3. five
4. trails
5. trains

A ram sat in the snow. That snow made the ram feel cold. The ram told five s_ea_ls that the snow is cold. Did that make the s_ea_ls mad? No. Those s_ea_ls like cold snow.

A ram sat in the snow. That snow made the ram feel cold.

That snow is cold.

Did that make the s<u>ea</u>ls mad? No.

We pl<u>ay</u> in cold snow.

p g w c

1. to
2. do

1. said
2. over
3. ask
4. snow
5. if
6. deep

1. needs
2. weeds
3. coats
4. trails

It is a cold day. Snow is in the stove. A cat and a rat feel cold. Is an ant as cold as the stove? No. That ant is in five coats.

It is a cold day. Snow is in the stove.

A cat and a rat feel cold. Is an ant as cold as the stove?

No. That ant is in five coats.

1. to
2. do
3. over
4. said
5. ask

1. more
2. mail
3. make

1. weeds
2. jokes
3. likes

1. go
2. pig

A mole and a rat like to play. The rat likes to play in the weeds. The mole likes to play jokes.

A mole and a rat like to play.

The rat likes to play in the weeds.

The mole likes to play jokes.

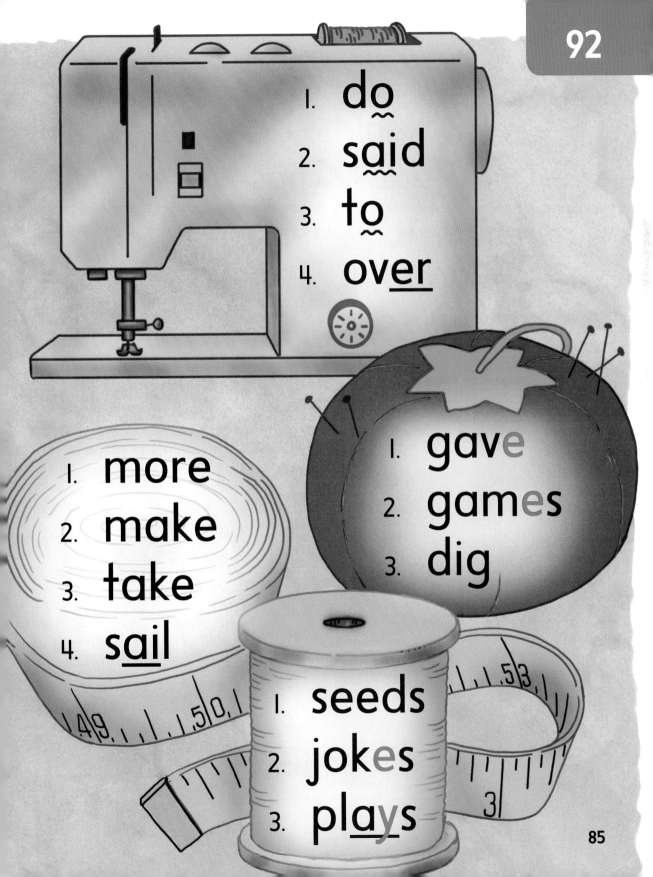

1. do
2. said
3. to
4. over

1. more
2. make
3. take
4. sail

1. gave
2. games
3. dig

1. seeds
2. jokes
3. plays

1. A mole said, "I play jokes."
2. A rat said, "Those jokes make me mad."
3. A ram said, "You play sick jokes."

I play jokes.

Those jokes make me mad.

You play sick jokes.

☆ c ☆ h ☆ g ☆ j ☆

1. wa̰s
2. do̰
3. nine
4. rats
5. t<u>oa</u>d

1. cave
2. came
3. c<u>oa</u>t
4. kick
5. kiss

1. sa̰id
2. we
3. slow
4. gave
5. go

An ant said, "I like to sit." So that ant sat. Five rats said, "We like to sit." So those rats sat with the ant.

An ant said, "I like to sit." So that ant sat.

Five rats said, "We like to sit."

So those rats sat with the ant.

1. he
2. hill
3. hide

1. wa̰s
2. do̰
3. to̰
4. s̰aid

1. pig
2. to͟ad
3. go͟at
4. came
5. m͟e͟an

1. pla͟y͟ed
2. lik͟ed

A mean ant was near a toad. The toad said, "Do you like to play?"

The ant said, "No."

The toad said, "Do you like to sleep?"

The ant said, "No."

The toad said, "Do you like to eat?"

The ant said, "No."

The toad said, "I do."

So the toad did that.

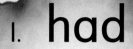

1. had
2. hate
3. hill

1. wins
2. go**a**ts
3. wav**e**s

1. cro**w**
2. green
3. r**ea**d
4. need
5. not**e**
6. fit

1. fill**ed**
2. s**ai**l**ed**
3. liv**ed**

A goat ate and ate. The goat said, "I feel sick."

A mole told the goat, "You need to sit and read."

The mole gave the goat a note to read. Did the goat do that with the note? No. The goat ate it.

I feel sick.

u   h   n   c   g

1. green
2. grow
3. coat
4. note
5. fit

1. had
2. hide
3. hid
4. hold
5. home

1. smiled   2. lived   3. sailed
4. filled   5. kicked

A crow had a green coat. A goat said to the crow, "I like that coat."

The crow said, "No goat can fit in this coat."

The goat said, "May I try?"

A crow had a green coat.

1. fit
2. green
3. crow
4. grow
5. gave

1. hike
2. had
3. has
4. home
5. hold
6. he

1. ask<u>ed</u>   2. kick<u>ed</u>   3. smil<u>ed</u>
4. kiss<u>ed</u>   5. lik<u>ed</u>

A crow had a green coat. A goat liked the coat. He said, "May I try that coat?"

So the crow gave the coat to the goat.

The goat said, "This coat will fit in me."

And the goat ate the coat.

May I try that coat?

The crow gave the c<u>oa</u>t t<u>o</u>
the g<u>oa</u>t.

98

1. us
2. run
3. up

1. hole
2. him
3. his
4. hikes
5. hate

1. was
2. do
3. said

1. lived
2. asked
3. hiked

The crow was cold. A ram was near. That ram had an old coat. The crow asked the ram, "Can I try that coat?"

The ram said, "This coat is for rams."

The crow said, "I can fit in that coat."

And he did.

The crow was cold. A ram
was near. That ram had an
old coat.

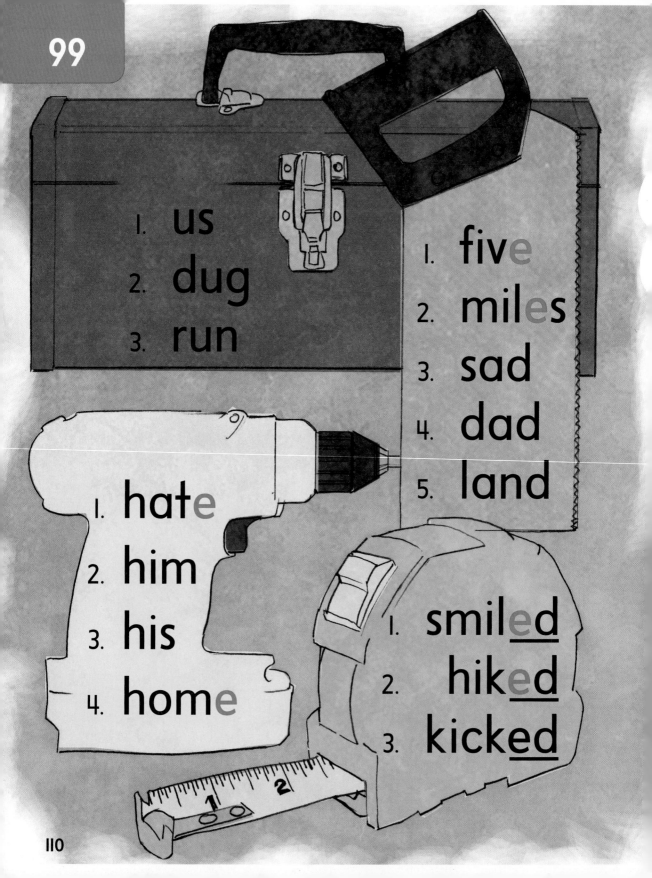

1. us
2. dug
3. run

1. five
2. miles
3. sad
4. dad
5. land

1. hate
2. him
3. his
4. home

1. smiled
2. hiked
3. kicked

A crow told his dad, "I hate to fly, so I will hike."

The crow hiked over five miles. That crow was sad as he came home. He told his dad, "No more hikes for me."

That hike gave him sore feet.

1. hug
2. run
3. up

1. w<u>a</u>s
2. t<u>o</u>
3. s<u>ai</u>d
4. d<u>o</u>

1. h<u>ea</u>r
2. hop<u>e</u>
3. greet
4. land
5. go
6. can

1. ston<u>e</u>s
2. mil<u>e</u>s
3. kiss<u>ed</u>
4. cav<u>e</u>s

An ant said, "I need to go home." It was five miles to his home. A crow said, "I can take you home. Hold my tail and we will fly."

In no time, the crow and the ant came over an ant hill. The ant told the crow to land. And the ant gave the crow a kiss.

102

1. fun
2. up
3. rug

1. into
2. was
3. stones
4. rides
5. caves
6. waves

1. leave
2. grass
3. hear
4. hole

119

A seal said, "I like to ride waves."

That seal was in waves near caves. The seal will ride a wave into a cave. The wave will take the seal over stones.

Will the seal like the ride? No. The ride will make the seal sore.

I will ride this wave into a cave.

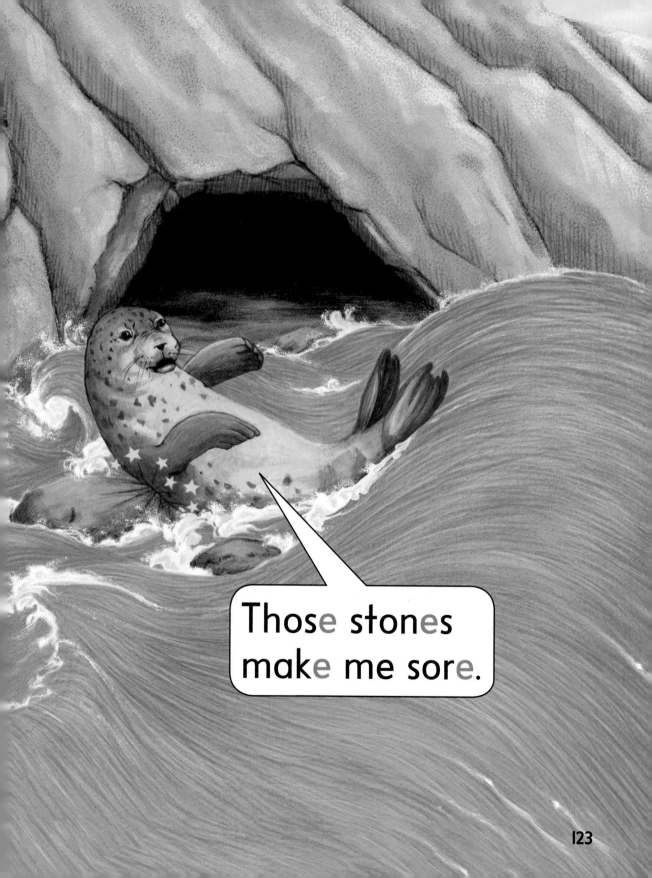

103

1. here
2. hole
3. l<u>ea</u>ve
4. st<u>ay</u>
5. slid
6. int<u>o</u>

1. mud
2. dug
3. sun

1. s<u>o</u>me
2. fr<u>o</u>m

A mole had a fine home. That home was in a hole. A toad came into the home. The mole said, "Leave my home."

The toad said, "No. I like it and I will stay."

The mole said, "If you stay, I will go."

And he did.

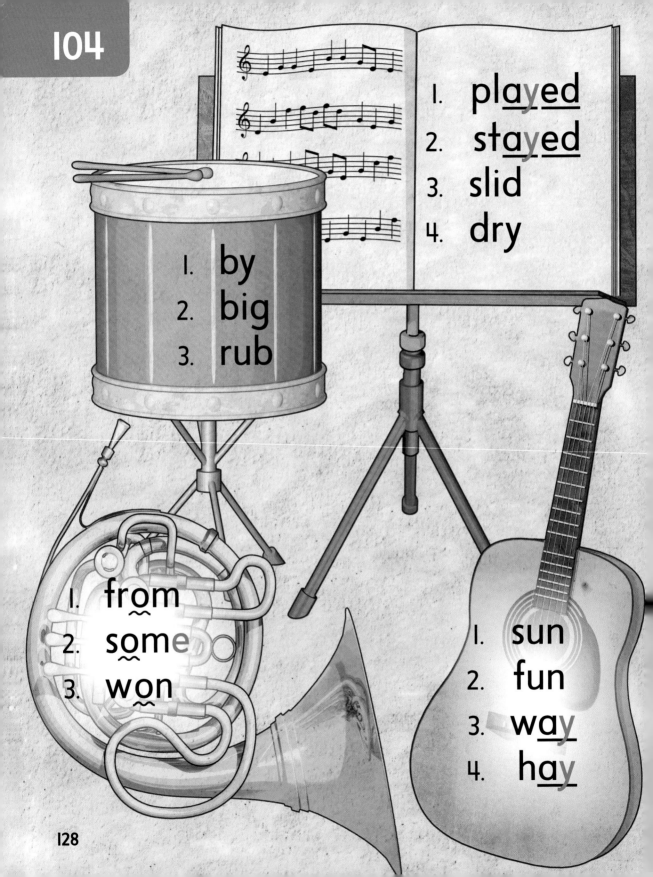

104

1. pl<u>ay</u>ed
2. st<u>ay</u>ed
3. slid
4. dry

1. by
2. big
3. rub

1. from
2. s<u>o</u>me
3. w<u>o</u>n

1. sun
2. fun
3. w<u>ay</u>
4. h<u>ay</u>

Five cats had fun at a lake. 2 cats played with a mole. 2 cats ran up a hill.

I cat slid into the lake.

Do cats like to play in a lake? No. Cats like to stay dry.

So the cat ran from the lake and sat in the sun.

Five cats had fun at a lake. 2 cats played with a mole. 2 cats ran up a hill.

I cat slid into the lake. Do cats like to play in a lake? No. Cats like to stay dry.

So the cat ran from the lake and sat in the sun.

105

1. but
2. big
3. grab
4. rub

1. some
2. said
3. was
4. do
5. from
6. into

1. hide
2. hid
3. hay
4. know
5. keep
6. named

A pig had a coat. The goat ate that coat. The pig said, "I am cold."

The goat said, "I know a way to keep the cold from you."

The goat told the pig, "Go to that hay pile and hide in it."

So the pig hid in the hay.

135

1. grab
2. dig
3. big

1. **of**
2. d**o**ne
3. s**o**me
4. c**o**me

1. pal
2. Al
3. nam**ed**
4. **t**ai**l**

1. stick
2. we
3. fly
4. kit**e**
5. thes**e**

An ant named Al told his pals, "We can fly."

These pals said, "No, no, no."

Al said, "Stay with me and you will see."

Al and his pals ran to a kite. Al said, "Grab the tail and we will fly."

The kite sailed over the trees. The ants said, "We can fly."

1. can't
2. didn't
3. don't

1. hav~e~
2. ask<u>ed</u>
3. last
4. but

1. stick
2. sick
3. tap~e~
4. dim~e~
5. mud
6. p<u>ay</u>

1. ~o~f
2. d~o~n~e~
3. c~o~me
4. fr~o~m

An old man asked a crow, "Will you pay a dime for a coat?"

The old man said, "No goat will eat that coat. It will stick to you."

The crow gave the man a dime. The man gave the crow a coat made of tape.

The crow said, "I can't fly."

The old man said, "But you can run." And the crow did.

144

145

1. can't
2. don't
3. didn't

1. Bob
2. hav<u>e</u>
3. ask<u>ed</u>
4. la<u>st</u>
5. by

1. but
2. mud
3. must
4. jump

1. come
2. of
3. from
4. done

The Hill of Mud
Part 1

Bob asked his dad, "Can I go for a hike with my pals?"

His dad said, "You may go, but you have to stay near the path. And you have to come home by five."

Bob and his pals hiked for 3 miles. At last a pal said, "I see a hill of mud."

More to come.

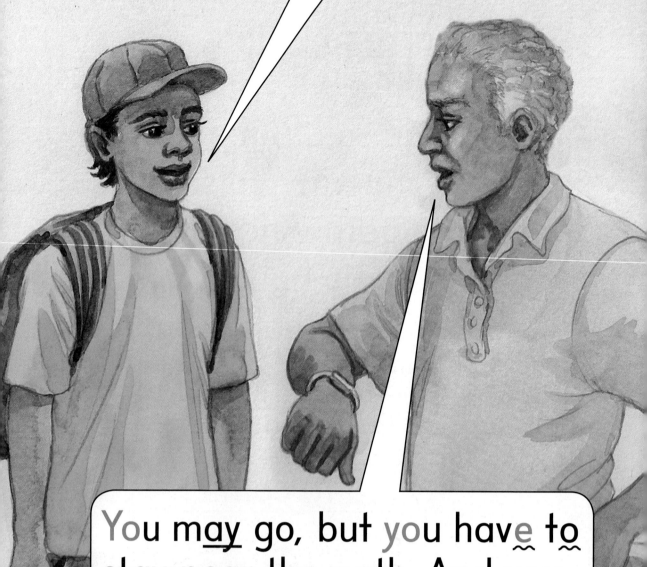

148

149

1. it's
2. didn't
3. don't

1. thing
2. these
3. big
4. be

1. other
2. have
3. of
4. ears
5. tears

1. stayed
2. played
3. fast
4. last
5. come
6. some

151

The Hill of Mud
Part 2

A pal said, "We can play in that big hill of mud."

Bob said, "But we have to stay near the path."

The pals said, "You stay. We will play."

But Bob didn't stay. He played in mud. At last some of his pals said, "It is time to go home."

Bob didn't hear his pals. Bob had mud in his ears.

More to come.